Easy
on the pocket
vegetable gardening
growing your own
groceries

DENNIS GREVILLE

Easy
on the pocket
vegetable gardening
growing your own
groceries

Published by

Hyndman Publishing

325 Purchas Road

RD 2, Amberley 7482

North Canterbury

ISBN 1-887382-36-1

TEXT & PHOTOGRAPHY

© Dennis Greville

DESIGN & ARTWORK

Dileva Design Ltd

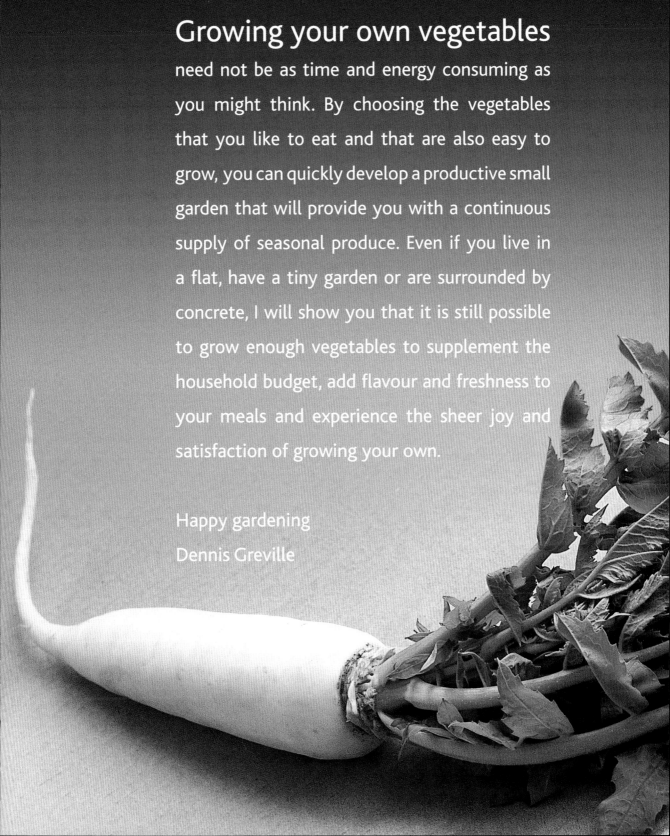

Growing your own vegetables

need not be as time and energy consuming as you might think. By choosing the vegetables that you like to eat and that are also easy to grow, you can quickly develop a productive small garden that will provide you with a continuous supply of seasonal produce. Even if you live in a flat, have a tiny garden or are surrounded by concrete, I will show you that it is still possible to grow enough vegetables to supplement the household budget, add flavour and freshness to your meals and experience the sheer joy and satisfaction of growing your own.

Happy gardening

Dennis Greville

Contents

Fresh is always best and what better way to ensure that your food is fresh, tasty and chemical-free than to grow your own.

By growing your own you can improve the nutritional value of your meals, and your vegetables and herbs are always at hand, just outside the back door. You can harvest just the quantity you need for a specific meal rather than being left with half a bag of tired lettuce leaves or shrivelled broccoli that ends up in the compost or in the rubbish bin.

Another practical benefit of growing your own vegetables is the economies you make by avoiding the usual costs of produce sold through retail outlets: here you are paying for expensive processing, packaging, transport and built-in wastage factors, as well as the inevitable profit margins associated with multi-tiered supply chains.

Growing vegetables at your place

First identify what you like to eat. A basic list might consist of a few favourite vegetables, your pick of salad ingredients and perhaps a few herbs. Depending where you are living you will need to consider key factors – local climate and weather conditions, and of course, the soil in your garden. These factors need to all come together in an equation that ensures you will get the best results from your vegetable plot given the range of plants that you have on your list.

In this book, my objective is to provide you with some clear guidelines on the preferred conditions for healthy productive growth of a broad range of our more popular edible plants, and a few more exotic, yet easy-to-grow options such as the winter-hardy mizuna, mibuna, and the daikon radish, which I believe are truly worth considering.

Things to consider

The keys to successful gardening lie in the planning and the location and preparation of the growing site, pot or planter soil. Don't underestimate the importance of good drainage, adequate moisture and a fertile well-prepared soil, without which few plants will flourish.

Consider carefully the types of vegetable that you want to grow. Some require full sun and perfect drainage whereas others will happily grow with less light and in a heavier soil.

To make the most of available space it is important to choose your plants and then map out where you will position them in your garden bed. Think about height of growth, spread of foliage, competition from adjacent plants for the essentials such as light, moisture, warmth and air.

Other frequently overlooked considerations are best planting times, growth time to maturity and how long your chosen plant will keep producing. Gardeners also often overlook the negative aspects of planting too many vegetables in a confined space. It is better to grow a few healthy and productive plants rather than a forest of stunted and unhappy vegetables that are simply unable to deliver delicious produce.

Starting from scratch

Starting with a grassy patch

A simple and cheap way to start a new garden is to remove the surface of the lawn by cutting thick turfs of about 30 x 40cm and 10cm thick. Cut them very neatly as these turfs will form the surrounding wall for the new garden. Untidy turfs will tend to fall apart as you stack them. Using a plank as your cutting edge will not only give valuable leverage for your spade but also ensure neat square turfs. A patch of grass 2m long by 1.2m wide is all you need to start producing your own crops.

Stack the turfs as you cut them from the soil to form a retaining edge for your garden. The optimum height of your wall should be about 30cm. Once you have cleared the area of grass and roots and made your edge all that remains is to fill the interior space with soil and compost. Dig the soil that you have cleared of grass, stacking each spadeful against the other.

Of course you will not have enough earth to fill the whole patch up to the top of the retaining wall, but with home-made compost and soil skimmed from other parts of the garden you can create a productive raised bed with little effort and practically no cost. The bed can also be filled by adding a variety of materials such as straw, kitchen vegetable scraps, well rotted sawdust (not chemically treated), leaves, weeds, coffee grounds or animal manure. By building up layers you can ensure that weeds and other less desirable materials are buried at the bottom of the bed where they can rot down to form valuable humus.

Well rotted animal manure isn't that easy to procure but if you have access to chicken or horse manure you can be sure that once it is added to the garden your leaf crops such as cabbage, silver beet, kale and broccoli will be the best around. Some animal manure can be full of weed seeds so it is advisable to rot it down in your compost heap before adding it to the vegetable garden.

You can also create a fertile garden bed by digging a 30-50cm deep hole, approximately a metre square. Fill it with garden, kitchen and any other organic waste that you can find. When the hole is full sprinkle the contents with blood and bone and then top the lot with the soil that you have removed from the hole. This process can then be repeated until you have a garden area of the required size.

Raised garden beds

You can also create a fertile garden from scratch without digging by enclosing an area of grass or soil using railway sleepers, large tree branches, punga logs, rocks, old masonry blocks, bricks or a simple timber frame clad with sheets of old roofing iron. Fill the contained area with layers of whatever organic material you can get you hands on and build up a humus-rich layer on the soil surface. Do this in the autumn, building the layers with fine sticks, leaves, clean sawdust, seaweed, and kitchen waste to a depth of approximately 30cm. Once you have created your blanket of organic waste sprinkle it with blood and bone and leave it to break down over a period of three to four months.

If you have the space another quick way to create a raised garden is to simply surround your chosen spot with hay bales and then fill the inside area with organic material. The bales give the plants shelter while the added organic material provides a fertile growing environment raised above ground level.

Raised gardens are another way of coping with heavy wet clay soils. A garden of rich friable soil is easy to plant and care for when it is raised above the troublesome, sticky clay. If bending low is a problem a raised bed can be a great advantage. Raised beds can also be attractive garden features.

The best raised beds that I have used are no wider than 1.2 metres. This makes sense particularly when you are tending to crops, weeding and harvesting, as it enables you to reach the centre of the bed from either side. Three or four raised beds 2-3m long and little more than a metre wide can be easily managed and should be sown or planted with forethought so that there will always be a succession of crops available for the table. Narrow beds also facilitate watering, hoeing, feeding, spraying and mulching. Raised beds to about 30cm will ensure that the soil remains warmer in the winter and spring.

Growing in containers

The restricted space of a small city garden or the limitations imposed by a tight balcony space are not valid excuses for living without the pleasures of freshly grown produce! You can create a productive garden using half barrels, wooden troughs, plastic and tin containers planted with a variety of well-chosen vegetables and herbs.

Containers are also ideal for busy families who don't have time for a large garden. A few large pots on the veranda or patio will readily provide generous quantities of fresh greens, tomatoes and herbs. For those with limited mobility and energy a few simple tomato plants, lettuces, and a potted basil, parsley or rosemary, conveniently located by the back door, should be sufficient to satisfy any craving for fresh vegetables. The transportability of container gardening also makes it a practical alternative if you are not permanently based.

Sun and shade are important considerations in a container garden. This is relevant when deciding what you intend to grow. Most vegetables prefer the sun but many will do equally well or better in part shade. Containers that are carefully sited to take advantage of summer shade offered by trees that are winter-deciduous effectively have the best of both worlds and are likely to produce excellent results.

Good soil preparation and constant moisture control are extremely important for all potted plants since they are unable to send roots out in search of food or water as do plants that grow in the garden. They also quickly deplete the soil in which they are growing and need constant feeding, care and attention if they are to produce to their best potential.

Soil-based, ready-made potting mixes are ideal for most plants and planting situations. They hold water well and usually contain a balanced supply of nutrients as well as water retaining crystals. They are also generally free of weed seed as well as soil-borne pests. All ready-made mixes now carry a warning against inhaling; nevertheless it pays to take care with all potting mixes, even homemade ones.

Your container should be large enough to ensure that the soil doesn't dry out between watering. Consider using a slightly larger container than may seem necessary and perhaps install a cheap and simple self-watering system to minimise daily maintenance. A timer attachment can easily be fitted to these systems ensuring plants are taken care of even when you forget or are away.

Mulching the surface of pots and larger containers with a layer of shingle, sawdust or compost will help to conserve moisture during the summer months. One good soaking every third day, depending on the heat of the day, will encourage roots to seek the bottom of the pot and make better use of available moisture. Wetting agents help ensure that moisture gets to the bottom of even the largest container. A capful of dishwash liquid added to several litres of water will achieve much the same result for a fraction of the cost.

Types of containers

Containers that are suitable for growing vegetables need to be large enough to accommodate your chosen plants and also be able to contain enough soil so as not to dry out when the weather warms and growth starts in earnest.

Choose the type of container to suit the vegetable that you want to grow. It makes little sense to plant moisture hungry, shade-loving plants such as parsley in tiny containers that are constantly exposed to the sun, or for that matter, sun-loving, deep-rooting plants such as pumpkins, carrots and potatoes in shallow pots in the shade.

Some vegetables and herbs will flourish in the special conditions that containers can provide. You can fill them with the soil type that your chosen plant prefers. A window box or hanging basket offers perfect conditions for plants that resent excessive moisture such as trailing tomatoes, strawberries, nasturtium or rosemary and sage. Mint on the other hand is best kept contained to prevent it from taking over the garden. A large tin can, sunk into the soil or old metal rubbish tin with the bottom removed makes an ideal prison for plants such as this that are invasive if allowed to spread into the garden.

Making your own containers

Wooden boxes

Wooden boxes are quick and simple to construct. With two equal sized sides and a base all you need do is add two end pieces and you will have a simple container that now needs little more than a few drainage holes drilled in the base.

Vermiculite (Worm casts, available from Garden Centres)

Vermiculite containers are also relatively simple to make. Make a basic mixture of three parts vermiculite, three parts peat moss and two parts cement and stir through. (It pays to wear a mask and rubber gloves when doing this.) Mix the dry ingredients with enough water to form cement that is the consistency of moist cottage cheese.

Most garden centres, even if they haven't got it in stock, will get vermiculite (expanded perlite) in for you. It is also available from centres that stock materials for hydroponic growing. Vermiculite is also a very good growing medium.

Free form

Create a mound of sand about the size of the pot that you would like to make and pour your mix onto the sand. Ensure that it is approximately 3cm thick, and lightly press a layer of chicken mesh into the mix as reinforcing. Ensure that the mesh doesn't extend beyond the edges of the pot. Place another 3cm layer of mix on top of the mesh and cover it all with a sheet of plastic and leave for at least two weeks before attempting any shaping or sanding. Vermiculite is easily shaped and sanded even when it is completely dry.

Mould

Place a cardboard box the size of the planter that you want on the ground outside with the opening facing up. To make the bottom of the trough, pour in a 3cm layer of your mix. Cut some chicken wire to the same shape as the box, 3cm smaller on all sides. Place it on top of the first layer of wet cement for reinforcement. Then top this with another 3cm layer of cement. Lightly smooth the surface to make it even. Create drainage holes by pushing several wooden dowels through the base. They can be removed when the planter has dried.

Place a smaller box upside down inside the larger box ensuring that the space between the boxes is about 6cm. Centre a layer of chicken wire between the inside and outside edges of the two boxes. The wire should be shorter than the mould so that it will not poke through when it is finished. Fill the space with the vermiculite mix and tamp it in with a dowel to ensure that all the air bubbles are removed.

Cover the trough with a sheet of plastic and leave for at least a fortnight. It is then a simple matter to pull away the inner box and tear the outer one away from the trough. Carefully remove the dowels and you will have a planter ready for use. The outside of the container can be easily worked with a wire brush to create an aged effect.

Improvising and using your imagination

While terracotta is still the first choice for many gardeners there are many alternative materials that do just as well when it comes to housing a few vegetables. I have used old tin cans (olive tins) or other tins with decorative surfaces to make

cheap, effective and interesting planters. Sometimes by adding a splash of paint you can give them extra character and interest.

Cane or plastic baskets neatly lined with plastic sheeting will not only give the container protection from moisture but also retain moisture inside the plastic liner, helping to keep the plants moist. An inexpensive basket from the market with a plastic rubbish bin liner can make an ideal growing environment. A few holes punched through the bottom of the liner will give all the drainage necessary. Three quarter, half or quarter barrels can be used to create a variety of planters of differing heights.

Old metal buckets, hollow pieces of driftwood, old hollowed tree stumps, car and machine parts - even old baths, spa pools, or washtubs - are just some of the many receptacles that you can use for growing your own vegetables. A hexagonal or round terracotta or concrete drainage pipe can also have wooden ends added to form a simple container, and drainage pipes stood on end in the garden also make suitable containers. Even a bag of compost can be cut open enough to let in the rain and planted. Remember to punch a few holes in the bottom of the bag to provide adequate drainage.

The possibilities are only limited by your imagination.

What to grow – and when

Seasonal selections

A lot will depend on your own local conditions as to just what plants are suitable for the various seasons.

SPRING: plant seedlings of artichoke, asparagus, beetroot, broad beans, broccoli, cabbage, capsicum, corn salad, cress, endive, leeks, lettuce, marrow, onions, peas, spinach, silver beet, tomato, basil and zucchini.

SUMMER: plant seedlings of dwarf and climbing beans, broccoli, beetroot, cabbage, carrots, cauliflower, celery, leeks, marrow, mustard, melons, New Zealand spinach, pumpkin, squash, silver beet, swede, sweet corn, tomato and zucchini.

AUTUMN: plant broad beans, beetroot, broccoli, brussels sprouts, cabbage, carrots, cauliflower, corn salad, leeks, winter hardy lettuce such as Cos, spinach, daikon radish, swede and turnip.

WINTER: harvest kumara before the soil becomes very wet and before the first frost. Plant broad beans, beetroot, broccoli, cabbage, cauliflower, corn salad, onions, parsley, peas, spinach and silver beet.

Growing your own groceries – a selection of the easiest vegetables

Maturity guide shown at the end of each vegetable. For shop bought seedlings to maturity generally deduct 30-35 days from the sowing times provided for each vegetable.

BEETROOT

Beetroot are easy to grow in pots or in the garden. The tender young beets can be plucked from the soil and eaten once they begin to swell. The leaves can also be harvested almost any time from germination to the harvest of the fully formed roots and added to salads or boiled like silver beet or spinach.

- Beetroot prefer to be sown or planted in a sunny and open site.

- A soil that has been well manured for a previous crop is ideal.

- Add lime to the soil at least several weeks before planting or sowing. Beetroot resent an acid soil.

- If it is the roots that you want then sow the seeds sparingly as every seed is in fact a group of seeds.

- The most succulent roots come from beet that have been kept moist particularly during the dry summer months.

- If you want the leaves for salads then scatter them thickly and harvest them by shearing with a pair of scissors. Try not to trim away the growing point of each tiny plant and you will get more leaves sprouting away.

- A sprinkle of general-purpose fertiliser will help to boost growth.

- Some beet such as the variety 'Bulls Blood' grow best in the winter: others such as 'Chioggia' grow best in spring and autumn. In the summer choose the richly flavoured 'Crosby's Egyptian Flat' or the long-keeping cylinder shaped variety 'Cylindra'.

Beetroot 50-60 days from sowing.

BROCCOLI AND CABBAGE

- Broccoli and cabbage are both easy to grow through the winter as long as they are well established when the colder weather arrives. Heading broccoli such as the 'Precoce Romanesco' type do better in cold areas whereas the more usual sprouting broccoli will grow successfully throughout a mild northern winter.

- When the plants of both broccoli and cabbage are developing they need plenty of nitrogenous fertiliser and as much well rotted compost as you can give them.

- Feed them with a liquid fertiliser when you plant them and then apply a liquid fertiliser every two or three weeks until the heads are fully formed and ready for picking. The simplest way to grow broccoli or cabbage is to buy a ready grown punnet of seedlings and plant them directly where you want them to grow.

- Broccoli and cabbage enjoy a lime-rich, moist, well-drained soil in full sun. Plant both in a sheltered sunny spot in a soil that has previously been used for a different crop. Nine plants at each planting should be enough for the average family.

Broccoli & **Cabbage** ready for picking 75-80 days from sowing.

CARROTS

- Sow seed thinly in a shallow drill 1cm deep and cover with light compost or a sandy soil mixture and space drills 30cm apart. Seed germinates readily and the plants soon need thinning.

- For best results sow carrots in well-worked, well-drained ground that has been heavily manured for a previous crop.

- Carrot seed must be sown very thinly, in rows, directly onto the ground where you want them to grow. The soil should be lightly raked over them and then pressed flat with the back of the rake.

- Carrots are susceptible to frost and unless you can offer them some protection they should not be sown until spring.

- Carrots mature in 10 – 12 weeks. Young thinned white carrots make a delicious and unusual addition to salads.

    Carrots mature 70 days from sowing.

LEEKS

Leeks are easier to grow than onions and can be plucked and eaten at any time once they have formed their cylinder-like stems. If you grow your own from seed the thinnings can be added to soups and salads to give their own unique flavour.

- Average soil is fine, but it must be free draining.

- Leeks like lime so I like to add several generous handfuls to the soil several weeks before either planting or sowing seed.

- Seedling leeks transplant easily when they are about 20cm high.

- Trim 8cm off the leaves and about 2cm off the roots before setting the seedlings out where they are to grow. Do this with plants purchased from garden centres although many will be already prepared, especially if you buy them in newspaper packed bunches.

- A dibber is a useful tool when planting out leek seedlings. A simple one can be fashioned by rounding off the end of a 50cm stick or piece of dowelling. This can then be used to make 15cm deep holes, 15cm apart in rows 30cm apart.

- Simply drop one plant into each hole and fill the hole with water to settle the roots. (You don't need to firm them into the soil).

- Until the plants are growing strongly keep topping up the holes with water. You can drop more than one plant into each hole. Although the resulting leeks will be smaller, the overall production will be about the same.

- If you want very white leeks then try blanching the stems by drawing soil up around them. Be careful to avoid soil dropping between the leaves as this makes cleaning them for the pot almost impossible.

- Cardboard tubes - even old toilet roll centres - can be dropped over maturing plants to achieve much the same result while avoiding the problem with soil spoiling your harvest.

- Leeks resent competing for light and moisture so it is important to keep them well weeded.

Leeks mature 75 days from sowing.

LETTUCE

Lettuce is an easy-to-grow leaf crop that, depending on the variety, can be harvested year round in many parts of the country.

- The soil should be rich in food. Well-rotted compost is ideal.

- Drainage must be good.

- A little lime added to the soil several weeks before planting would ensure strong and healthy growth.

- To grow the most succulent lettuce there should be no check in growth. The leaves of plants that are starved of food or left to dry out will become tough and bitter.

- In a cooler garden where drainage is a problem try growing lettuce in a pot or raising the planter bed. As long as plants are kept moist they will flourish in such conditions.

- Choose the right variety for the season in question. 'Drunken Woman', 'Rouge d' hiver', 'Vivian' and 'Cos' are all good varieties for winter growing. 'Webb's Wonderful' is heat resistant and slow to go to seed, making it an ideal summer and autumn variety. 'Black Seeded Simpson' matures early, producing a full-sized, bright green head with slightly crinkled leaves. It is very adaptable and withstands heat, drought, and light frost. 'Red Batavian' and 'Iceberg' are slow to bolt and produce crunchy sweet green hearts.

   Lettuce 30 days baby leaf, 60 days fully mature.

MIZUNA

Easy to grow in the winter and spring, mizuna can provide salad greens for months on end. The mustard flavoured leaves are delicious when mixed with lettuce and any other salad herbs.

- Dig the soil deeply. Ensure that it is well drained.
- Plant in a rich soil that has been well stocked with compost from a previous crop.
- Add a little lime a few weeks before planting.
- Take care when planting not to bend the taproot.
- Keep plants growing quickly. Do not allow them to dry out.
- Feed with a liquid fertiliser to boost growth.
- Pick regularly by cutting leaves from the base of the plant.

   Mizuna 35 days from sowing.

PEAS

- Peas need a cool root run.
- Choose a variety that suits your climate and season.
- The soil should be fertile and well drained.
- A little lime may need to be added to the soil a few weeks before sowing.

- Sow seed shallowly and cover with netting to protect the seeds from birds and the sprouting seedlings from birds as well as slugs and snails.

- Provide support of strings and bamboo sticks.

- Keep water to a minimum until the plants flower, then water regularly onto the roots.

- Pick the crop as often as possible. The more that you pick the more you will get.

Peas ready 55 days from sowing.

POTATOES

- Potatoes are divided into early, early main and main crop varieties. It pays to choose varieties that suit not only your soil but also the season. 'Cliff's Kidney' is an early crop potato best planted in early spring, 'Arran Banner' an early main, and 'Rua' a main crop potato that is best planted in late spring or early summer.

- Potatoes like the warmth and need covering with frost cloth when frost threatens.

- They also prefer a soil that is well drained and fertile.

- Plant deeper in the colder months, more shallowly in spring and summer. You can choose to add a potato fertiliser in the bottom of the trench. Placing a length of paper under the tubers prevents them from burn and gets plants off to a good start.

- Earth the plants up when you get the time. This is important to create better and bigger tubers.

- Potatoes can be planted in a barrel or a car tyre. In such a confined space earthing up is made easier.

- Ensure that plants have plenty of moisture especially when they begin to grow strongly.

Potatoes 90-120 days from planting depending on season and variety.

PUMPKINS

If you have the room or even a fence that the vines can climb on, pumpkins are not only easy to grow but also easy to accommodate. I have grown them along fences and have been astonished at how the vines can carry the very heavy fruit without collapsing.

- The site should be sheltered from cold winds and open to the sun.
- If you want to get ahead of the seasons, sow seeds inside in pots for planting out when all danger of frost has passed. Don't sow pumpkins until both the soil and the weather have warmed in early summer.
- The soil should be rich in organic matter.
- A little lime added a few weeks before sowing might be necessary on acid soils.
- Plants need to be well watered especially in summer when they are setting fruit.
- Good drainage is essential.

  Pumpkins 100-120 days from sowing.

RADISH

What could be simpler to grow than a radish? The French breakfast varieties will germinate in a few days given the right conditions and within a month will be producing a crop that can be used in salads or cooked much as the Japanese daikon and other radishes are. The ball shaped radish Rabu is very tasty, quick growing and also good cooked or in salads.

- Sunny sites are best.
- In hot weather you can grow radishes in part shade.
- Keep the ground moist at all times. A well-drained soil is essential.
- Fresh manure does not suit radish growing.

  Radish 25 days from sowing.

RUNNER BEANS

Always expensive and always soft and rubbery when you find them in shops? Why not grow your own? As long as you have a few bamboo poles to form a tepee-like structure or a handy north-facing fence that you can cover with chicken wire or some similar support then you can have fresh beans for the summer and early autumn. You can even grow beans in a container if you can ensure that the soil never dries out.

- Runner beans like a deep loose soil. They also like plenty of compost incorporated into the soil.
- Add a little lime a few weeks before planting.
- Tie carefully until the plants are climbing freely.
- Water weekly from the first flowering. A good soak once a week is better than the occasional splash of water.
- Mulch plants with compost, well-rotted sawdust or well rotted seaweed.
- In most of the country treat them as annuals by cutting the vines back in autumn and leaving the roots to re-sprout the next spring.
- In very cold regions mulch the roots heavily after they have been cut back or treat them as annuals.

   Runner Beans 55-60 days from sowing.

SILVER BEET

This plant is easy to grow and able to survive the winter weather in many parts of the country.

- Plant in a sunny and open site for best results. Silver beet will grow readily in a container.
- The soil should be both fertile and well drained.
- Add a little lime to the soil several weeks before planting allowing time for it to work into the soil.
- Chicken manure or a fertiliser with a high nitrogen content will boost growth and produce large lush leaves.

- Keep plants well weeded as they grow. Silver beet resents being crowded by other plants.
- When the weather is warm and dry silver beet needs plenty of moisture to prevent it from bolting to seed.

Silver Beet 55 days from seed.

SPINACH

- Choose the variety that best suits your climate and season.
- Spinach likes to grow in a soil that has been enriched with plenty of well-rotted compost.
- Provide plants with good drainage otherwise they will fail.
- Spinach likes to have a cool root run so it pays to mulch the surface of the soil around the plants with compost, sawdust, straw or something similar.
- Water your plants well in warm dry weather.
- When harvesting, break the leaves away carefully from the base of the plant.

New Zealand spinach is very drought resistant and will flourish where many other varieties will fail.

- It has much the same requirements as ordinary spinach.
- It is tolerant of dry conditions and will grow in poor soils.
- New Zealand spinach also grows well in pots and containers.

Spinach 40 days from seed, **NZ Spinach** 35-40 days from seed.

TOMATOES

- Tomatoes are easy to grow and require full sun and shelter from strong winds. Space plants 40-50cm apart. The small cherry types can be grown in pots or even in hanging baskets and require very little care once they are established.

- Seedling tomatoes can be raised in trays for planting out when the spring days are warm and settled. Having them ready for planting enables you to get them in as soon as the days warm.

- Often it is easier to buy them as established seedlings from your local garden centre and nurture them until planting time. Plant seedlings at least 40cm apart. * Tomatoes, especially the smaller varieties such as 'Tommy Toe', 'Sweet 100' and 'Tumbling Tom', grow well in containers or planter bags.

   Tomatoes 84 days from seed.

ZUCCHINI

- Zucchini like to grow in a sunny sheltered site.
- They do best in a soil full of rich compost.
- Although they like plenty of moisture when the fruit is forming they also like good drainage.
- Avoid watering the leaves and the fruit. Apply water directly to the root zone either with a drip hose or flood the soil carefully especially in dry weather.
- When they are growing vigorously, side dress plants with compost with a little blood and bone mixed in.
- Pick fruit when it is small. They are delicious eaten raw, added to salads or cooked.
- Compact upright varieties such as 'Gold Rush' or the climbing variety zucchini 'Rampicante' are ideal where space is limited.

   Zucchini 45 days from sowing.

Baby leaf salads

There are many seeds that are suitable for sprouting or for baby leaf production. The types that are best for sprouting include alfalfa, mustard, green broccoli, red cabbage, lentils, mung bean, onion, radish, red clover, snow peas, rocket, Italian parsley and chickpea.

Baby leaf production is best obtained from mass sowing seeds of mizuna, mibuna, silver beet, beetroot, cress, amaranth, kale, varieties of mustard, cress, rocket, mange-tout peas, radish, watercress and the well known mesclun mix that includes a variety of spicy herbs and greens including corn salad, endive, rocket, mustard, chicory, lettuces, pak choi and a variety of beets.

Baby Leaf Salads 30 days from sowing.

Crops that go on and on

Kale, endive tres fine maraichere, Florence fennel, lettuce Vivian, miners lettuce (a real spreader), mizuna and mibuna, arugula, plantago, New Zealand spinach, spinach, shingiku, silver beet, broccolini - the sprouting broccoli – are just some of the many crops that produce over a long period. Many herbs such as rosemary, sage and thyme will also produce over a very long season with rosemary flourishing in the winter and spring.

A few easy-to-grow exotic vegetables and herbs

Corn salad is very easy to grow and makes a delicious addition to winter salads. It will grow in cool conditions and can be harvested by plucking a few leaves when the plants have produced five or six leaves.

Corn Salad 35-40 days from sowing.

Mibuna and **mizuna** are some of the easiest winter greens that can be grown in almost any climatic conditions during the cooler months. Both these plants

thrive in full sun and a rich soil and should be sown or planted in late summer or early autumn. Both are members of the cabbage family and can be boiled or added to stir-fries.

Globe artichokes are not difficult to cultivate if they have the advantage of a rich well-drained fertile soil in full sun. They can be grown in pots as can the so-called root or Jerusalem artichoke. Jerusalem artichokes on the other hand flourish when they have plenty of moisture but also need good drainage. Their autumn flowering alone makes them well worth growing.

> **Globe Artichokes** 90-100 days. However, seed grown plants do not usually produce flowers (edible heads) in the first year.

Mexican Coriander (eryngium foetidum) is a perennial version of the more generally known annual variety. It is favoured where the true coriander (coriandrum sativum) does not do well because it can stand humid summer weather. The leaves are tough, but if they are sliced finely or ground with garlic and ginger are delicious. Mexican coriander dries well, retaining flavour and colour and can also be added to cooked dishes where it will impart its own special flavour.

> **Mexican Coriander** 40 days. Plants are perennial and are best planted from division of established plants.

Florence fennel is another delicious salad green that is not only easy to grow but also has a long season. Depending on the variety grown you can have it producing from spring until autumn. 'Milano' is recommended for spring and early summer sowing. 'Orion' is better for the late summer and early autumn.

> **Florence Fennel** from sowing to harvest 75-80 days. Mature plants do not usually produce flowers (edible heads) in the first year.

Sprouting broccoli or **broccolini** produces masses of tender side shoots quite unlike the more usual variety. These shoots can be harvested when they are needed without cutting a full head. Broccoli 'Tender Stems' is very similar to broccolini. 'Purple Sprouting Early' is both prolific and very hardy. I have seen it almost frozen and then miraculously bounce back. The tasty side shoots are a rich purple-blue in colour.

> **Sprouting Broccoli** or **Broccolini** sowing to harvest 80-85 days.

Growing your own berries

A fertiliser with an NPK of 10: 9: 8 is ideal for all established berry crops.

- Keeping them well fed and well watered, especially when the fruit is forming, is essential for a bountiful crop.
- Well-rotted compost is ideal for most berries and a dressing of super phosphate will also help to boost growth.
- A high potash feed (such as tomato food) scattered at the base of the plants will help to ensure a good harvest.
- For most berry crops the fruit will need to be covered with nets as they ripen to fend off the birds.

STRAWBERRIES

Strawberries grow best in a soil that has been well broken up and filled with organic matter. Well-rotted compost is ideal and a dressing of superphosphate will help boost growth. Choose a warm, open sheltered site and ensure that the bed is well drained.

Planting times vary throughout the country with many growers preferring to have plants settled in before the coldest months of winter, while others prefer to wait until spring.

Set plants at 30cm intervals with rows 75cm apart. Roots should be spread carefully ensuring that the crown of the plant is not buried. Keep the bed moist and cut back any runners that appear before the flowers form. Boost growth with liquid manure in the late winter and early spring and surround the plants with pine needles, straw or black plastic to keep the fruit clean and the plants moist. Strawberry runners are an ideal source of new plants if the parent plants are healthy and vigorous. Each runner has a series of little plants attached and these can either be pegged into the soil until they are growing strongly or if they have already formed roots, cut free and planted in a moist soil.

Strawberries – plant divisions in late winter and they will be producing by early summer.

RASPBERRIES

Raspberries are easy to grow and tough, preferring cold winters, mild summers, and shelter from strong winds which reduce soil moisture, lower temperatures and discourage bees. In thorny varieties, wind also damages foliage and fruit.

Raspberries grow to 1.5 metres tall and wide and do best in a slightly acid well drained but moist soil. A generous dressing of compost and superphosphate will help keep plants moist as the fruit develops and will ensure a good crop. The berries are produced from mid summer until autumn depending on the variety. 'Autumn Bliss' is a good cropper as are 'Everbearer', 'Willamette' and 'Taylor'. After picking, cut all the canes that have fruited to the ground leaving only the fresh ones that have developed in the new season's growth.

Raspberries – plant canes in winter or early spring for summer fruit.

Seasonal timing

It is important to plant or sow at the right season otherwise the resulting crop will be disappointing – see the following 'Vegetables Year Round Guide'. Choose varieties that suit your climate and season, and check with your local plant centre if unsure.

Aubergine, peppers, kumara, cucumber, sweet corn, tomatoes, New Zealand spinach, basil and all the melons including pumpkins, need frost free conditions to flourish as they are not cold hardy. Plant them indoors in pots if there is the slightest chance of a cold snap. Plant them out only when the weather is settled and warm. Broccoli, cabbage, winter lettuce, onions, peas, potatoes and spinach are relatively hardy and less sensitive to the cold.

Successional sowing and planting

By choosing your sowing times carefully it is possible to extend your harvesting season. If you want to provide vegetables over a long period make plantings at 14 day intervals. This is particularly important for crops such as peas, beans and radish that have a short peak period. Peas and beans are best sown en masse so that you can have them in abundance.

Planting half a dozen lettuces every three weeks from late winter will ensure that you have fresh salads almost all year round. Choose some of the more winter-hardy varieties such as 'Canasta', 'Corcade', and the attractive 'Red of Winter' ('Rouge d'Hiver'). This also applies to many other vegetables where mass cropping is not convenient or practical.

Vegetables Year Round Guide

Spring	Sow / Plant	Harvest	Note
September	Artichoke, tuberous artichokes, asparagus crowns, aubergine, beetroot, broad beans, broccoli, cabbage, carrots, capsicum, celery, corn salad, garlic, kale, leeks, lettuce, mustard, onions, peas, parsley, parsnips, early potatoes, spinach, silver beet, tomatoes, turnips.	Asparagus, beet, beetroot, broad beans, broccoli, cabbage, leeks, parsnips, silver beet, corn salad, kale and turnips.	This is a busy month preparing the soil. If you have planted green fertiliser crops such as mustard, oats, broad beans, and lupin now is the time to dig them in. This should be done at least six weeks before planting into that area.
October	Broccoli, cabbage, carrots, leeks, lettuce, early potatoes, radish, silver beet, tomatoes. Basil seeds need a warm place under cover until they are large enough to plant out. Plant seeds of the following herbs: caraway, coriander, dill, marjoram, rosemary, tarragon and thyme.	Broccoli, beetroot, broad beans, cabbage, carrots, corn salad, lettuce, parsley, early potatoes, spinach, leeks, silver beet.	This is a very busy month for the serious vegetable gardener. Ensure that the soil is well drained and warm before sowing seed otherwise it will rot.

Spring	Sow / Plant	Harvest	Note
November	Beans (dwarf and climbing), beetroot, broccoli, cabbage, celery, carrots, cucumber, lettuce, parsnips, melon, pumpkins, potatoes (early and maincrop), radish, silver beet, tomatoes, zucchini.	Beetroot, broad beans, broccoli, cabbage, celery, carrots, leeks, lettuce, potatoes, onion thinnings, radishes, silver beet.	This is another very busy month in the vegetable garden. At this time of the year growing conditions are optimum and plants will grow quickly. Check watering systems and mulch the soil with straw, sawdust and compost as temperatures rise and the soil begins to dry out.

Summer	Sow / Plant	Harvest	Note
December	All beans, beetroot, broccoli, cabbage, carrots, leeks, lettuce, parsnips, potatoes (maincrop), pumpkins, radish, silver beet.	Broad beans, broccoli, cabbage, carrots, dwarf beans, lettuce, onions, potatoes (early crop), radish, silver beet, tomatoes.	As the soil begins to dry careful attention should be paid to weeding, watering and mulching. Make sure that the soil is moist before mulching or much of the benefit will be lost.

January	Beans (both dwarf and climbing), beetroot, broccoli, cabbage, capsicum, carrots, kumara, lettuce, leeks, potatoes, radish, silver beet, sweet corn, tomatoes and zucchini.	Beans, broccoli, cabbage, carrots, celery, cucumber, garlic, lettuce, potatoes, radish, silver beet, tomatoes and zucchini.	Watering and weeding are important activities at this time of the year. Cultivate with a push hoe and keep the garden moist. Succulent salad vegetables need water if they are going to deliver.

Summer		Sow / Plant	Harvest	Note
	February	Beetroot, beans, broccoli, brussels sprouts, cabbage, carrots, cauliflower, celery, cucumber, lettuce and radish.	Beans, broccoli, cabbage, carrots, cucumber lettuce, onions, potatoes (early and mid season varieties), radish, silver beet, tomatoes, zucchini.	Keep newly planted seedlings covered and moist at least until they are established. More weeding, watering and mulching is essential if crops are to reach their potential. Liquid fertiliser applied now will greatly boost growth as will side dressing plants with compost or a little blood and bone.

Autumn		Sow / Plant	Harvest	Note
	March	Beetroot, broccoli, cabbage, cauliflower, cress, leeks, lettuce, parsnips, radish, peas, silver beet, spring onions, swede turnip. In warm areas, beans (climbing and dwarf).	Broccoli, beetroot, cauliflower, cress, cabbage, carrots, lettuce, potatoes (maincrop), radish, silver beet, tomatoes.	Protect crops from insect infestation that usually coincides with dry weather and a slow down in the garden growth. Weeding, watering and removing spent crops so that the winter crop can be put in place occupies much of this month. Build a new compost heap with the debris from the garden.

Autumn	Sow / Plant	Harvest	Note
April	Broad beans, broccoli, cabbage, cauliflower, leeks, radish, winter lettuce, onions, silver beet, spinach. Plant herbs such as lavender, mint, rosemary, savoury and thyme.	Beans, broccoli, cabbage, capsicum, carrots, lettuce, potatoes (maincrop), pumpkins, radish, silver beet, tomatoes.	Start a new strawberry bed by digging the ground over thoroughly and working in plenty of compost and blood and bone. Soil that is becoming vacant from spent summer crops can be dug over, fertilised and left for a month before replanting with winter crops.
May	Broad beans in well drained soil, broccoli, cabbage, carrots, cauliflower, garlic, lettuce, onions, parsley, radish and spinach.	Broccoli, cabbage, capsicum, carrots, lettuce, potatoes, pumpkins, silver beet.	This is the season of harvest. Once crops are cleared and stored or frozen, dig the soil over and if it isn't going to be used through the winter try planting a green fertiliser crop of mustard or lupin.

Winter	Sow / Plant	Harvest	Note
June	Broad beans, endive and garlic. In sheltered warm areas, cabbage, carrots, broccoli, lettuce, spinach and turnips can still be sown.	Broccoli, cabbage, carrots, garlic, parsnips, rhubarb crowns, shallots, silver beet.	The garden is beginning to wind down for winter. Now is a good time to make a plan for next year's garden. Ensure that seedlings are protected from slugs and snails. They seldom seem to sleep!

Winter	Sow / Plant	Harvest	Note
July	Broad beans, broccoli, cabbage, garlic, lettuce, onions, radish, shallots, spinach, upland cress, but only if the soil is well drained.	Broccoli, cabbage, leeks, parsnips, silver beet, mustard, mizuna, winter lettuce in mild areas.	Begin to dig in any green crops that were planted in autumn to help improve the soil. Don't wait until the plants have become large. It is easier to dig them in when they are still relatively small.
August	Aubergine and capsicum seed in seed trays for planting out in mid spring. Broccoli, cabbage, endive, garlic, leeks, lettuce, parsnips, rhubarb, silver beet and turnips.	Broccoli, cabbage, leeks, parsnips and silver beet, lettuce, mustard.	Keep making and adding compost to the garden. Compost greatly improves soil while at the same time boosting the health of your plants. Prick out tomato seedlings into individual pots once they are growing strongly. Resist planting them out into the garden until the days are warm and settled.

Seeds and Seedlings

When buying seedlings it is best to choose those that are well spaced, upright and healthy in colour, free of leaf blemishes and of vigorous appearance. It also pays to check them carefully for any mould, or insect and soil pests. Avoid seedlings with any sign of wilt in the leaves or stems. Crowded seedlings are already weakened by competing in their trays and are therefore unlikely to flourish and reach their potential.

Some garden centres offer a good selection of top quality vegetable seedlings but if you want to try some of the more unusual varieties it may be advisable to start your own from seed.

How to raise your own seedlings from seed

It is generally best to start seed in seed trays or pots. A good quality seed raising mix is essential if you want healthy vigorous plants. Firm the soil into the container making sure that the soil surface is level. Soak the seedbed, let it drain and then sow the seed. Press seeds into the soil and cover the tray with a double sheet of newspaper and then with a pane of glass or clear plastic. This will retain moisture, provide shade as may be necessary and encourage germination by retention of warmth. Set the container in a warm light spot, out of direct sunlight. Check each day until the seed germinates. Remove the plastic or glass and paper once all the seed has sprouted.

Firm the soil and water it well before sowing.

Using a folded piece of paper will make sowing seed easier. Cover lightly with soil once sown and water again.

Pricking out – seedlings pricked out into a pot.

Thinning and transplanting

Thin your seedlings to allow sufficient space for strong plants to develop. You will need extra trays for this exercise. Transplanting is a delicate process, as careless handling will cause damage to the young plants, which are unlikely to recover. Avoid disturbing the roots and don't compress them into the soil when re-planting because you may tear or choke them. Firm the soil lightly giving the plant just enough support to stand upright and continue its development.

As seedlings germinate, water them well with a liquid fertiliser (see 'Plant Foods: making your own' page 59). When planting seedlings, first make a small hole, being careful not to compact the soil. Fill the hole with water or diluted liquid fertiliser. This moistens the area in which the young roots will grow. Place the seedling in the hole and gently firm the soil around it.

Shade the young plants from excessive heat of direct sunlight until they become established. If plants dehydrate after planting they seldom thrive.

If the weather is hot and the soil dry, many newly-planted seedlings will bolt (go to seed). To prevent this, select varieties that are slow to bolt and plant them in part shade, keeping the soil evenly moist at all times – refer to 'Problems, Pests & Diseases' page 63.

Seed saving

Many seeds are best sown fresh. Usually ripe seedpod heads turn brown or black as they dry out and start to split. Lettuce, rocket, cabbage, spinach, sweet corn and even potatoes produce seed that is well worth collecting especially if the varieties are not hybrids.

By watching when the first seeds start to fall you will know when they are ready to collect. Paper bags are ideal for collecting seeds. Once collected I like to spread them out in the sun for an hour or so to ensure that they are bug free. They can then be put back in their respective bags and hung up in an airy, shady place to dry for at least a week. When you are certain the seed is dry, sieve it and remove any debris that may have got in with the seed, then pour the clean seed into labelled envelopes. To keep the seed dry, a teaspoon of silica gel (cobalt chloride) placed in a cloth bag inside a sealable container with your various seeds will do the trick.

The seeds of fleshy vegetables such as tomato, cucumber, capsicum, chilli, melons and pumpkin are also relatively easy to collect. Simply split or cut the vegetable and remove the seeds, placing them on absorbent paper. Once they are dry store them in paper bags. Seeds that have stuck to the paper can either be prised off or stored paper and all, until planting time.

Avoid hybrid varieties if you want to save your own seed; these will only give disappointing results if you save them year after year. Hybrid seed seldom comes true to the parent plant, so seed saved from hybrid varieties produces many different plant types that can and often will be disappointing to the home gardener. Some seed may even be sterile. In the main hybrids have been bred with an emphasis on yield at the expense of flavour and hardiness. Non-hybrid seed has been selected for hundreds of years for flavour and vigour.

Organic seed

In New Zealand only a few companies offer a selection of certified organic seed to the public. If you are serious about organics then get a seed catalogue from King Seeds, Katikati. IFOAM, the international body for organics and agriculture, verify this. 'Erica Vale' seed, imported from England, offers a large selection of organic vegetable seed including heirloom and hard-to-find varieties and is available from some garden centres. Yates offer a small organic seed selection that is also available through most garden outlets nationwide. 'Niche Seeds' of Ashhurst, Manawatu also offer certified organic seed. A catalogue is available at most garden centres.

Various organic food outlets around the country also sell seedlings raised from organic seed.

How much seed do you need?

A little seed goes a long way. If you are given to heavy handedness then why not try seed tapes. Simply break off the required length of tape containing the number of seeds that you require and then place it in the soil. This method ensures that you only sow what you want and what's more the resulting seedlings are perfectly spaced without the need for time consuming thinning. Six or seven healthy seedlings are better than 20 spindly weak ones!

Sowing tiny seeds can be made much easier by mixing them with fine dry sand or by sprinkling them from a folded piece of stiff paper. This way, they can be carefully controlled and scattered precisely into seed drills or over the soil surface.

As few as 6 or 7 pumpkin plants will be more than many gardens can accommodate when they are fully-grown. Pumpkin, squash, kumi kumi, zucchini, melon and butternut seeds can either be sown directly where you intend them to grow or into tiny pots for planting out later when they have germinated. Sow three seeds into a mound of compost placed on top of fertile soil. Once they germinate remove all but the strongest seedling. In small gardens many of the trailing varieties of pumpkin and melon can be trained along fences, so taking up as little space as possible.

Requirements and conditions

Climate and microclimate

If you have an exposed site open to prevailing winds you will need some form of windbreak. This calms the wind and also raises air temperatures within the enclosed space, allowing plants to flourish more readily. You can make an effective, cost free and attractive sheltering wall by neatly cutting turfs from the lawn and stacking them to form a wall. In colonial times this method was used effectively to create both garden shelter and animal-proof barriers.

Brush panels, shade cloth and fences can all be quickly constructed. For a longer-term solution you might consider planting a quick, low-growing hedge of sage, upright rosemary and lavender, or the larger growing hebe, flax, grisilinea, phebalium or pittosporum.

 Some vegetables, particularly salad greens, grow best in part shade rather than full sun. Lettuce, lamb lettuce, chicory and rocket won't tolerate the burning rays of the sun, particularly in summer. Salad greens will become tough and bitter if they are grown in full sun. Leaf vegetables such as lettuce, silver beet, broccoli, mustard and cabbage are generally more tolerant of the shade than those that need to fruit and flower such as tomatoes and pumpkins. Root vegetables such as carrots, potatoes and beetroot will tolerate a little shade but require at least half a day of full sun to thrive.

Leaf vegetables have another added advantage for gardeners in that they can be picked and enjoyed at almost any stage from baby leaf to maturity. The shady spots in the garden are particularly useful for growing and harvesting vegetables in mid to late summer when the sun is at its hottest. A simple bamboo screen or a piece of shade cloth tacked to a few overhead beams may be all that you need to ensure that your summer salad crops remain sweet and tender.

In corners of the garden where the summer or winter sun refuses to shine try placing a mirror where it can reflect at least some of the sun's light and warmth. It may be necessary to shift the mirror from time to time to ensure that you make the most of the sun's warming rays as it moves throughout the seasons. Don't forget that you may need to remove it in the summer months!

The Soil

Soil preparation is always important and turning it with a spade or cultivating the soil with a hand fork, even in a pot, allows air and water into the plants' roots. These elements work together to loosen compacted non-productive ground. By adding compost and fertiliser – preferably organic – it is possible to build a fertile environment that will produce disease-free, health-giving vegetables.

Soil texture and structure is an important consideration when you are deciding what crops to plant. Plants growing in sandy soil must be watered and fed frequently, because soil that is too sandy dries out quickly and cannot retain fertiliser. On the other hand, the loose coarse structure of sand provides the aeration necessary for good root growth. Heavier soil such as clay holds water and nutrients well but usually has poor drainage.

In order to improve the qualities of your soil it may be necessary to add fertiliser and materials such as compost that will help retain water in sandy soils, and when added to clay soil, will make it coarser, more airy and faster draining.

Loosening your soil provides plants with growth, stimulating air to their roots. To loosen heavy soils digging in sand, rotting sawdust, animal manure, compost, fine gravel, even ash from your fireplace (preferably untreated wood), will provide a rich source of humus as they begin to rot down. The determined use of gypsum or dolomite year after year will also help.

Where soils are light and free-draining, digging in a heavy compost will increase water retention. By adding a mulch of compost, well rotted grass clippings, sawdust or other organic materials such as coffee grounds, almost any soil can be encouraged to produce abundantly.

Adding untreated sawdust will gradually build up a layer of friable mulch on top of the soil. This layer will greatly benefit shallow rooting plants and short-lived annuals. However it is more effective when it is dug in and incorporated well into the soil.

What to do with clay

Improving clay soils is challenging, particularly if they are low lying and wet. You may need to dig trenches and lay drains to partially dry out heavy and wet clay soils, or you may choose to raise the beds above the soil surface.

Dig and break up clay soils in the spring as they begin to dry out. The time to do this is limited as these types of soil change quickly from soft and wet to dry and hard in a matter of weeks. Digging clay soils in the winter is likely to do more harm than good.

Clay soils are cold and wet during winter and spring but they can be warmed up and dried out to some extent by covering with heavy-duty plastic sheeting. This will enable you to begin planting out earlier to take full advantage of the peak growing season. Once warmed up, clay soils hold their heat longer than sandy ones.

The best time to apply manure, sand, compost, lime, gypsum or other clay improvers is when the soil begins to warm in the early spring. Work a small area at one time rather than tackling the entire vegetable garden. Most clay improvers are slow to show results and will require regular application to be effective. Digging them in is the best way to ensure they work to greatest effect.

Adding gypsum does not affect the pH of the soil and can be safely used with all plants and in all soils. It makes compacted clay soils more friable and crumbly and allows plant roots deeper penetration. Dig gypsum well into the soil. Water in well if soils are dry - you will notice the difference almost immediately. The fine, flour-like particles are surprisingly gritty and begin to improve aeration and drainage immediately. In heavy soils up to 2kg per square metre should be used. Gypsum can also be combined with compost thereby accelerating break down and becoming more quickly integrated with the soil.

Lime is important to healthy gardens but must be applied carefully because not all vegetables tolerate it. Earthworms flourish in lime-rich soils and their presence will encourage healthy plant growth. Lime works slowly and should be dug in thoroughly. Adding a combination of lime, compost and other organic matter will considerably speed up the break-down of heavy clay soils so that they provide a better growing medium.

Adding sand and gravel to the garden will gradually help break up heavy clay soils and enable plant roots to derive essential food and moisture. Like many clay improvers they are most effective when they are dug well into the soil.

Quite frankly compost is the most effective and cheapest soil improver (refer to 'Successful Composting', page 55).

Watering

An effective watering system needs to be considered carefully. Water plants thoroughly and deeply after planting to settle the soil around the roots and promote deep root growth. Pay especially close attention to watering in the first few weeks while plants develop their root systems. Allow the soil surface to dry before watering again. While moisture is essential for the growth of most perennials, many also require perfect drainage.

Drip irrigation is an ideal watering method for many potted plants as it avoids wetting the leaves and flowers and applies a little water just where it is needed.

Roof top gardens dry out quickly and all plants left for prolonged periods without moisture will die. Provide only what your chosen plants need and ensure that any surplus moisture can drain away freely without dripping onto the balcony below and possibly destroying neighbourly relations.

- Conserve moisture by adding compost to the soil.
- Water crystals (crystal rain, etc) and products such as Saturaid allow the soil to absorb and conserve moisture. They are ideal in sandy soils and also for use in pots and planters.

- Leaves, sawdust, grass clippings – in fact anything that covers the soil – will prevent moisture from evaporating and allow your plants to make full use of it.
- A simple summer technique to make watering easier is to group plants that like a lot of water and those that prefer less together in groups, rather than spreading them out in rows. Pot grown herbs and vegetables can also be grouped together for easy watering.

Mulching

Mulch is simply a protective layer of material that is spread on top of the soil.

Mulching enriches and protects the soil and acts as an insulator to ensure that plant roots stay cool in summer and warm in winter. Mulches can be organic - such as grass clippings, coffee grounds, newspaper, sawdust, straw, bark chips, and similar materials - or inorganic material such as stones, brick chips and sheet plastic.

Both organic and inorganic mulches are useful in the garden and help to protect the soil from erosion, reduce compaction from heavy rains while also conserving moisture, maintain a more even soil temperature and suppress weed growth. Mulch also keeps vegetables clean and free from splashes of soil.

Compost

Successful composting – organic soil additions

Compost is one of the best natural soil conditioners and is created when organic waste materials rot. The rotting process involves bacterial microorganisms which help to create ideal growing conditions. All soils benefit from the addition of compost or well-rotted manure.

Compost is always valuable so it pays to make as much as you can. You can make your own easily from kitchen and garden waste but you do need at least two or even three bins at least a metre square if you want a constant supply for the garden. If you simply haven't got the time and space to make your own there are many growing mediums that can be readily purchased from your local garden centre.

Tips for making quick compost

1   Use a large container at least a metre square. Large containers produce more heat increasing the rate at which the material will rot down.

2   Keep the heap moist at all times.

3   Cover the top in wet or cold weather to prevent it from becoming saturated and cold.

4   Let in plenty of air by using layers of light twiggy material between layers of soft leaves and kitchen waste.

5   To speed up the process of decomposition fork the heap out after three weeks and turn it over putting the old material from the outsides back into the middle. A light dressing of dried blood or blood and bone added in between the layers would also speed the process up.

If you are short of space try chopping up all your compost material into fine pieces and then put them into a black plastic bin liner. Mix in some blood and bone, dried blood or animal manure and add enough water to wet the mix evenly through. Punch a few holes in the bag and tie it at the top. Put the bag in a sunny warm spot under a hedge or some other part of the garden where it won't be in the way turning it over every few weeks. In a few months you will have usable compost.

Soil mixes

It is important to note that all commercial soil mixes can contain harmful microorganisms. They should not be opened in enclosed spaces and you should use gloves whenever you are handling these mixes. If you do need to use soil mixes in the greenhouse then it pays to wear a mask.

Black Magic seed raising mix is nutrient enriched so you don't need to add anything other than seed. It contains a controlled release fertiliser and absorbs water quickly. Yates Black Magic is ideal for raising seeds in trays and is also suitable for outdoor seed sowing directly into the ground. It is easy to re-wet and keep evenly moist because it contains a unique wetting agent, which allows the mix to absorb water quickly and uniformly, distributing it evenly to the roots.

Patio and tub mixes are produced by many companies. Most claim to be the complete outdoor container mix for tubs, troughs and pots. I often find that many are a little light for our hot dry summers and like to add topsoil from the garden to give the mix more bulk. Specially blended from peat moss, bark and pumice these mixes provide a free draining mix with high moisture retention. Many tub and patio mixes are specially formulated with a controlled release fertiliser for easy feeding, providing plants with a safe, balanced and continuous supply of nutrients plus trace elements for eight months or even longer.

Manures and plant foods

Green manures

Lucerne, blue lupin, mustard, broad beans or oats can all be sown liberally in the mid autumn with the intention that they will later be dug in before maturity to provide a valuable source of compost. This procedure will not only improve the texture of the soil but also raises the humus level. Last autumn I sowed mustard and used the leaves for salads all winter. Recently I dug it in to replenish the soil.

Plant foods – making your own

Liquid fertilisers watered on roots or sprayed on leaves of your plants will help to boost growth within a brief period.

1 **Willow water:** Young seedlings will benefit greatly if they are dipped in willow water. This is made by simply soaking green willow foliage in water for a few days. Gather several handfuls of willow twigs and leaves, cover with warm water and leave overnight or for several days. This brew can also be kept in a jar with a tight-fitting lid where it will remain effective for several months. Water your plants with willow water to boost growth or soak them in it overnight before planting. Cuttings of herbs and other plants dipped in willow water will also root more quickly than those that are not.

Willow water contains salicylic acid that boosts growth by helping to trigger a plant's natural defences against bacteria, fungi and viruses while at the same time stimulating root formation. Commercial rooting preparations contain a synthetic form of this acid, found naturally in the leaves and twigs of willows. Any willow (Salix) tree will work.

2 **Aspirin** also contains salicylic acid. Dissolve 3 aspirins in 15 litres of water and pour or spray this mix onto your vegetable plants to boost them. There is no need to resort to artificial growth boosters or chemical pesticides.

3 Soak **grass clippings** in a bucket of water and leave to ferment. This mix smells terrible while fermenting so keep it well away from the house. This brew is especially effective when watered on to the roots of tomato plants once they have started growing vigorously and have set their first flowers. A little dried blood added to the soil at this stage will also bring excellent results to all your vegetable plants.

4 Simple **liquid manures** for the garden are really easy to make. Try soaking fish remains, bird, cow, horse and pig manure, and seaweed in a covered bucket or tank of water for a few weeks. The resulting brew smells terrible and in warmer weather is likely to attract clouds of flies. Dilute your brew to the colour of weak tea by adding more water and apply to the roots of your plants avoiding contact with the leaves to avoid leaf burn and also for health reasons. You should water in the brew after application. This will assist uptake of nutrients by the plants and also avoids risk of residual smell. By adding more water to the original material you can re-use it several times, before it loses its beneficial value.

In the case of quick growing salad crops you'll probably notice the difference within days of applying a liquid food.

To keep fertilisers from burning roots and leaves always apply to moist soil and wet leaves and avoid using in the heat of the day.

5. **Herb teas** are another cost-effective way to boost the health of your garden. Pick as much St John's wort, sage, basil, thyme, nasturtium, chamomile, or nettle as you can spare. Don't mix your herbs unless you have insufficient of one kind! Cover with water and bring to the boil. Remove the tea from the heat and let it cool for at least an hour. You can use the tea directly on your plants or dilute it with 3 parts of water. Apply immediately after preparation, as the beneficial properties do not last.

Chamomile and St John's wort (hypericum) tea are most beneficial if they are applied to the roots of herbs and vegetables when they are being planted.

Stinging nettle is rich in iron. Water basil and tomatoes with nettle tea for best results.

If nettle tea is sprayed onto plants they will be strengthened and better able to withstand drought. Try growing basil and tomato plants together and watering with nettle tea for best results.

Sage tea is a great growth stimulant for established plants.

Problems, Pests and Diseases

Bolting to seed

Bolting can be limited by planting out young, healthy plants that have not been stressed from lack of moisture or food. It can also be avoided by maintaining a steady, moderate rate of growth and even temperatures throughout the growing period. Watering well when transplanting and gently firming into the soil to remove any air pockets that might form around the young roots will also help to avoid bolting as will planting suitable varieties at the correct time for your area, supplying a rich fertile soil and not subjecting plants to competition from weeds.

Slow to bolt varieties include the variety of silver beet known as 'Silverado', and 'Slo Bolt Silver beet'. Arugula, the wild Italian rocket is slower to bolt than ordinary rocket, and lettuce 'Great Lakes' and 'Webb's Wonderful' are both bolt resistant. The 'Giant Red Mustard', and perpetual spinach are also slow to bolt.

Chinese cabbage such as bok choy is best sown where you want it to grow. If you do need to transplant it do this with great care as shifting will often cause immature plants to bolt to seed.

Pests and diseases

Early identification is usually the first line of defence against pests and diseases. Other defences include crop rotation, choosing resistant cultivars, sowing only certified clean seed and tubers, as well as controlling weeds, applying sufficient fertiliser and water.

Treating the garden gently makes particularly good sense if you want to establish a healthy natural environment. Spraying with harsh chemicals may well solve the immediate problem but can in the long term upset the delicate balance of nature. Once the right proportions are restored pests gradually become less troublesome. This doesn't mean that the garden will ever be without some troublesome insects but with careful control they will cause a minimum of damage.

Plants that are neglected, underfed, and left to dry out won't grow as vigorously as those that are watered and fed regularly and become more susceptible to diseases such as rust, mildew, leaf spot and insect pests. Seedlings subjected to prolonged dry periods and temperature changes will suffer stress and damage to their root systems that also exacerbates the spread of disease.

If you don't like the idea of using toxic sprays in the garden then you may like to entice birds into your garden by supplying them with a daily apple, regularly scattering breadcrumbs, or making a suet-based bird pudding. Birds in the garden will quickly and naturally remove many pests.

Another method of insect control is to plant spearmint, tansy, pennyroyal, nasturtium and garlic in the vegetable garden to control ants and aphids. White cabbage butterfly and many other insects dislike sage, rosemary, thyme and mint. Interplanting crops with aromatic plants like garlic, chives, or marigolds can repel many problem insects.

Slugs and snails are a common problem in many gardens. Where the winters are wet and mild these pests will multiply quickly causing a lot of damage particularly in the spring garden. Copper tape can be used to protect trees and plants from slugs and snails. Slugs and snails have a sense of smell and usually travel at night in search of succulent green leaves. They can be repelled by a mulch of bark or oak leaves, and wood ash, wormwood tea or lime sprinkled around vulnerable plants will often cause the slugs and snails to lose vital moisture and die.

Of course if rainfall is high many products are washed away before they can be effective. In such circumstances it may be necessary to form nighttime vigilante parties carrying buckets of salty water and simply pick the pests off infested plants and drop them in to drown. The remains can be added to the compost heap.

Pyrethrum sprays are available that will control ants, aphids, thrips, caterpillars, whitefly and many harmful insects on indoor plants and in the garden. These natural garden remedies are ideal for organic gardeners but even then it is usually recommended that you wait at least a day after spraying before eating vegetable and citrus crops. For some pests like aphids and caterpillars, a strong spray from a garden hose can also knock them loose. It's important to spray the underside of the leaves where most insect pests reside.

Sticky yellow traps have been specially designed to attract flying insects such as white fly, aphid, leaf miner and thrip. These traps attract small insects by the use of coloured pigments, without the use of chemicals. A non-drying adhesive traps the insects and is specially suited for enclosed areas such as greenhouses and enclosed growing areas. Non-chemical lures can be used to protect apple and pear trees from codling moth (cydia pomonella) damage. These pheromone lures attract the male moth with the scent used by the female — once in the trap they are unable to escape from the sticky base. One trap is usually enough to provide effective control for five trees. These traps are harmless to pets, bees and beneficial insects.

Homemade garlic or hot pepper sprays can protect young seedlings from slugs, snails, aphids and other insect pests.

Crop rotation and good garden sanitation is important if you want to get control over many garden pests. Don't be tempted to grow the same crop in the same place year after year especially if there have been problems with specific diseases. Heavy feeding plants such as cabbage, cauliflower and all leaf vegetables as well as cucumber, pumpkin, sweet corn, rhubarb and tomatoes should be planted immediately after fertilising the garden with compost and well rotted animal manure. These heavy feeders should be followed by legumes such as peas and beans, which act as soil improvers by adding nitrogen to the soil through their root nodules. The legumes should be followed by light feeders such as all root vegetables including carrots, beet, radish, turnip and parsnip.

Organic Anti-Fungal Spray

To prepare the spray, combine

1 Tbsp of cayenne or hot chilli pepper

1 onion and 6 cloves of garlic minced

1 tsp pure soap (not detergent)

5 litres hot water

Blend and let sit for 1–2 days. Strain and use as a spray. Ground cayenne or red hot pepper can also be sprinkled on the leaves of plants (apply when leaves are slightly damp) to repel chewing insects or added to the planting hole with bone meal or fertiliser to keep dogs and cats away from your plants. This is most effective in the morning when leaves are moist with dew. Spray vulnerable plants with this mix at least once a week and especially after rainfall.

The best solution to pest problems, however, is maintaining sound garden practices like building healthy soil, rotating crops, and cleaning up your garden at the end of the season ensuring that no diseased fruit remains on the soil and that insect pests don't have handy piles of decayed vegetation left where they can winter over until the next season.

Weeding

If you have ever despaired about those weeds that seem to spring up in the garden as soon as the warm weather arrives, take heart - you are not alone. For centuries gardeners have sought to control the rampant weed growth that results from having a fertile, moist, warm garden.

Perhaps the easiest way to control weeds is to ensure that they never seed! Even if you don't have time to weed, take a minute or two to tear off any seed heads that might appear in the summer and autumn, before they can scatter and colonise the garden. Of course the ideal solution is to use a fork or hoe to uproot weeds when they are still young and their root systems are still shallow. All it takes is a few moments' work. Weeds that are left to become well established take a real effort to remove. The trick of maintenance weeding is to tackle the task a little and often rather than leaving weeding until the situation becomes desperate.

If you have the time, then hand weeding is the only really satisfactory way to deal with weeds, especially in the vegetable garden. 'Wonder Weeders', a kitchen fork and knife are all useful aids when it comes to clearing the garden so that you can grow the plants that you want. A simple push or torpedo Dutch hoe is another quick and effective way to deal with small weeds.

For tough weeds I always prefer to use a spray-free alternative. In fact I am reluctant at any time to use chemical sprays, especially with edible plants. In cases of extreme weed growth a machete or a petrol driven or powerful electric weedeater can be used to knock off the top growth and then it's a relatively simple matter to dig and turn the soil ready for planting.

Chemical pesticides are not the only way to reduce the problems caused by pests and diseases - in fact you can protect your garden naturally by using lots of safe, non-toxic products. Following is a useful chart to help you decide which approach is right for you.

Remedies for common insect pests and fungal diseases

Controlling Insect Pests

Along with seasonal abundance in the vegetable garden, there comes a parallel increase in activity in the insect kingdom. If the problem is a minor one, you may take the position that we can spare a few morsels for the odd bug or bird. More serious infestations will require treatment if crops are to remain healthy. Listed below are both inorganic and organic remedies for common insect pests.

Aphids

Aphids cause plants to lose vigour and collapse. Shoots are stunted.

ORGANIC TREATMENT:	Ladybirds, waxeye (silvereye birds), parasitic wasps, and fungal diseases are good control agents. Soapy water, 'Neem Oil' Pyrethrum sprays or garlic spray are also effective. Watch carefully in the spring for the first signs of infestation.
INORGANIC TREATMENT:	Systemic insecticides such as 'Mavrik' are very effective. Mavrik will kill insect pests yet will not harm the bees.

Beetles (bronze, green etc.)

Beetles will strip plants of their leaves and devour flower buds.

ORGANIC TREATMENT:	Garlic sprays will deter them momentarily (see recipe on page 75). Shake them into a bucket of water that has a few drops of kerosene added. As a preventative, encourage plants to grow healthily and rapidly using foliar feeding.
INORGANIC TREATMENT:	Apply an insecticide spray.

Carrot rust fly

Young plants suffering from a carrot fly invasion will wilt, while older plants will show signs of burrowing.

ORGANIC TREATMENT:	Companion planting with onions, leeks, rosemary and sage will deter these pests. Use a succession of sowing dates so that some sowings will miss the peak egg laying flights of the carrot fly.
INORGANIC TREATMENT:	Sprinkle Diazanon ('Soil Insect Killer') granules in the seed drill as sowing proceeds. Spray with Target.

Caterpillars and leaf rollers

Caterpillars and leaf rollers will eat leaves and flower buds, and deposit droppings on leaves. Left to their own devices they can decimate a crop of cabbages.

ORGANIC TREATMENT:	Remove by hand or dust with Derris Dust (or flour from the kitchen).
INORGANIC TREATMENT:	Use an insecticide such as 'Mavrik', or Derris Dust with carbaryl added.

Cutworms

Cutworms shelter under plants during the day and come out to feed at night. Seedlings will suddenly fail, having had their stems eaten through.

ORGANIC TREATMENT:	Keep the soil free of weeds and apply an oak leaf mulch. Several parasitic wasps and tachinid flies may control cutworm larvae.
INORGANIC TREATMENT:	Spray with a suitable insecticide.

Mealy Bug

This pest has an oval body covered with white waxy threads. They are often found on indoor, balcony and greenhouse vegetables and ornamentals.

ORGANIC TREATMENT:	Wash the plant down outside with the hose. Use a soft brush dipped in a 50/50 methylated spirits and water mix to dislodge any determined bugs. Keep plants well-fed and healthy, and use a garlic spray.
INORGANIC TREATMENT:	A systemic spray such as Orthene or 'Confidor'.

Mite

Mites are tiny insects that attack young buds, causing them to contort and twist.

ORGANIC TREATMENT:	Keep plants moist in the summer and spray the undersides of the leaves with water. Pick off and burn the first signs of this pest.
INORGANIC TREATMENT:	A miticide such as 'Mavrik' or 'Super Shield'.

Red spider mite

These are tiny mites usually found on the undersides of leaves. They become bright red in the late summer and autumn, and flourish in hot dry conditions.

ORGANIC TREATMENT:	Keep plants and the surrounding area sprayed with water. Pick off and destroy the first signs of this destructive pest.
INORGANIC TREATMENT:	Use a miticide like 'Mavrik'.

Scale

Both hard and soft scale are rapid breeders. Both forms exude a sticky honeydew that attracts ants. A scale attack will debilitate and eventually kill a plant.

ORGANIC TREATMENT:	Remove manually or use a toothbrush dipped in a weak solution of vinegar, oil and water.
INORGANIC TREATMENT:	Apply an insecticide spray with a little horticultural oil added at summer strength.

Slaters

Slaters can do minor damage to crops.

ORGANIC TREATMENT:	Remove sheltering places such as rotting leaves. Regular cultivation of the soil will help.
INORGANIC TREATMENT:	Carbaryl will deter them but will kill earthworms.

Slugs and snails

Slugs and snails can do major damage to crops, and are especially hazardous to small seedlings. They are persistent and destructive garden pests.

ORGANIC TREATMENT:	'Quash' is a natural product and safe with animals. Crushed egg shells or sand placed around young seedlings will help protect them from slugs and snails. In severe cases trap them in stale beer in dishes, or in an upturned pot, or crush by hand and foot. Remove as much rotting vegetation as possible from the garden. This will eliminate breeding and hiding places.
INORGANIC TREATMENT:	'Mesurol' or similar bait.

Sooty mould

Sooty mould is a tiny insect which feeds on the secretions of mealy bugs, scale and aphids. It appears on leaves as a dark soot-like mould, hence its name.

ORGANIC TREATMENT:	Garlic spray or soapy water.
INORGANIC TREATMENT:	'Mavrik' with a little 'Conqueror Oil' added, or 'Orthene' or other general garden insecticide.

Spittlebugs

Spittlebugs are common in spring and early summer. The insects form frothy bubbles that can be unsightly, but they do the garden little harm.

ORGANIC TREATMENT:	Regular hosings are often sufficient to keep the numbers down.
INORGANIC TREATMENT:	Hose the plants down first to get rid of the spittle froth, then spray with an insecticide like 'Mavrik'.

Thrips

Thrips are very small brown or black insects which feed on the sap of many plants. Foliage becomes silvery and dehydrated.

ORGANIC TREATMENT:	Garlic spray. Keep plants healthy by regular, even feeding. Water regularly. Pick off and destroy any infected leaves as soon as the pest is seen.
INORGANIC TREATMENT:	'Orthene', 'Gild' or Maldison.

Whitefly

Tiny, white and moth-like. Unsightly and destructive sap-sucking pest.

ORGANIC TREATMENT:	Garlic spray, 'Neem Oil' and regular sprayings with soapy water.
INORGANIC TREATMENT:	'Target' or 'Orthene'.

Treating Fungal Diseases

Much can be done to reduce the incidence of fungal disease by choosing disease-resistant plant varieties. Check the seed packets for information.

Blight

Blight appears on tomatoes and potatoes in warm, humid weather in mid to late summer. Leaves become distorted and the plant begins to fail.

ORGANIC TREATMENT:	Use a garlic spray and remove any diseased leaves and burn them. Keep a free flow of air around plants by removing lower foliage in the case of tomatoes. Mulch with seaweed. Rotate crops and sprinkle a little lime under plants.
INORGANIC TREATMENT:	Regular spraying with a copper based spray (such as 'Champion Copper') or a fungicide.

Damping off

This causes plants to sulk, refuse to grow, and then wilt and collapse at ground level.

ORGANIC TREATMENT:	Avoid overwatering, use sterilised soil and keep a good airflow around plants.
INORGANIC TREATMENT:	A copper based spray, or 'Thiram'.

Downy mildew

This mildew attacks cucumbers, leeks, lettuces, onions, peas, pumpkins, spinach and swede, especially when the weather is erratic.

ORGANIC TREATMENT:	Keep airflow circulating by removing excess foliage. Do not overcrowd when planting. Destroy affected area at the first signs of the disease. Use garlic spray.
INORGANIC TREATMENT:	Spray with a copper spray, 'Bravo' or 'Super Sulphur'.

Powdery mildew

Powdery mildew attacks when the soil is dry and the air is humid. The leaves and skins of cucumbers, marrows, melons, and pumpkins are covered in a white powdery coat. Even silver beet leaves can be affected.

ORGANIC TREATMENT:	Space plants so that the air can move freely. Rotate crops. Keep the soil moist during dry periods. A spray made of a weak vinegar solution helps. Flowers of sulphur sprinkled on the leaves is also useful.
INORGANIC TREATMENT:	Use a fungicide spray such as 'Bravo', 'Saprol', 'Green Guard' or 'Yates Fungus Fighter'.

Rust

Rust is a difficult disease to control. It can destroy crops of beetroot, broad beans, garlic and leeks. Brownish orange spores form on infected plants.

ORGANIC TREATMENT:	Remove and burn all infected leaves as soon as they appear. Mulch the soil heavily with sawdust or seaweed. Rotate crops to prevent re-infection. Avoid using heavily nitrogenous fertiliser. Use rust resistant seed.
INORGANIC TREATMENT:	Copper sprays or weekly sprayings of 'Saprol'.

Garlic Spray

Garlic spray is a useful organic weapon against some insect pests. It is easy to make. You will need:

2 whole heads of garlic
    (approx 10 cloves each head)

1 teaspoon kerosene

1 litre of water

1 tablespoon of grated pure soap
    or Lux soap flakes

To prepare the spray:
Crush the garlic and mix with the kerosene. Boil the water with the soap flakes until they are dissolved. Cool, add the garlic and kerosene mixture, and strain. Keep this mixture in a sealed jar until you wish to use it. Dilute the mix at a ratio of 1 to 50 parts of water before applying to the garden. Omitting the garlic and substituting the boiled liquid from 12 rhubarb leaves can make a similar spray.

Companions

Many gardeners use companion planting. Plants growing together in the small space of the average garden interact with one another. A tall growing species gives shade, thus protecting shade loving plants while at the same time suppressing other low growing sun loving plants. Other plants interact by simply competing for food or water. It has also been discovered that many plants release excretions into the soil through both their leaves and roots. Some plants find these excretions toxic while others thrive in such an environment. By choosing and planting good neighbour plants together, many problems can be avoided ensuring better flowering and heavier crops.

Good Companions

- **Asparagus** like to grow with **tomatoes**.
- **Beans** and **celery** like to grow together.
- **Broad beans**, intercropped with **spinach** makes good sense. Both plants are beneficial to each other.
- **Carrots** grown with **onions**, **sage** and **rosemary** are said to be free from attacks by the carrot rust fly.
- **Dill** attracts bees that aid pollination. A row of dill on either side of a patch of **corn** makes both plants grow stronger and bear more heavily.
- **Elderberry** assists fermentation of the compost heap.
- **Foxglove** strengthens all plants growing in its vicinity.
- **Garlic** grows well with **roses**.
- **Herbs** are beneficial in the **vegetable** garden.
- **Jerusalem artichoke** not only produces delicious roots but also has colourful golden flowers in the autumn.
- **Kohl rabi** grows well with **beets** and **onions**.
- **Lavender** and **silver beet** grow well together. Lavender is a useful plant to have in the garden. It attracts bees and raises the level of beneficial aromas in the garden.

- **Leeks** and **celery** grow well together.

- **Lettuce** grows well with **strawberries** and **marigold**. The French marigold (tagetes) excretes a substance into the soil that limits the spread of harmful soil nematodes. **Marigold** and **tomato** associate well also.

- **Mint** will help to repel the white cabbage butterfly caterpillar.

- **Nasturtiums** planted near **broccoli** will keep aphids away. They help **radish** and benefit **potatoes** when planted with them. Nasturtium makes an excellent herb tea for both spraying as well as watering onto plants.

- **Oak leaves** make an ideal compost and mulch for **strawberries**.

- **Onions, garlic and parsley** make ideal companion plants for **roses**. The perfume of roses is stronger when planted with any member of the onion family.

- **Parsley** also grows well with **tomatoes** and flowering parsley attracts bees into the garden.

- **Pumpkin** and **beans** grow well together. Corn, pumpkins and beans are wonderful neighbours. Early planted corn provides shelter while at the same time providing a structure for beans to climb on. Pumpkins benefit from shade provided by these taller growing neighbours.

- **Radishes** help most **vegetables** growing near them. **Chervil** and **radish** are particularly beneficial.

- **Rosemary** and **sage** will flourish when planted together. Sage tea is an ideal growth stimulant for established plants.

- **Sage** is good grown with **cabbages**. It helps to keep the white butterfly at bay. Sage tea is an effective liquid fertiliser for established plants.

- **Sweet basil** and **tomatoes** enjoy being grown together. A rich moist soil suits them both. The highly aromatic nature of both these plants makes them great companions so try growing them together and watering with nettle tea for best results.
- **Valerian** in the vegetable garden aids most vegetables in its vicinity.
- **Wood ash** that is untreated is a useful addition to the **compost heap** or vegetable garden.
- **Yarrow** in the vegetable garden helps all plants growing near it. It also makes a good tea for watering onto young seedlings.

Bad Companions

- **Parsley** and **mint** will soon choke each other out and die. Keep these two herbs apart if you want them to thrive.
- **Strawberries** like to grow with **beans**, **lettuce**, **spinach** and **borage**, but plant them with tomatoes and neither plant will do well.
- **Dill** and **carrots** should not be grown together; **dill** sown with **carrots** greatly reduces the crop.
- The **dandelion** exudes a substance that inhibits the growth of neighbouring plants, but made into a herb tea or used in the compost it has a beneficial influence on plant growth.
- **Poppies** are beautiful in the vegetable garden, but they rob the soil of its nutrients. After growing them for several years in the same place feed the soil with compost and fertiliser before planting with a different crop.
- **Potatoes** will not yield well when grown with **spinach**, **orach** or **fat hen**, all close relations.
- **Gladiolus** and **peas** or **beans** will not grow well together.
- **Sunflowers** and **potatoes** are bad neighbours which can stunt each other if grown together. The **sunflower** is a greedy crop and will soon deplete the soil.
- **Tulips** suppress **wheat** growth.
- **Tomatoes** and **potatoes** resent **walnut** trees and their acidic leaves.

Managing your time – time-saving tips

- Be realistic as successful gardens take time and regular attention. Keep your garden small yet productive.

- Check your vegetable garden every day to notice what is happening. Ten minutes every day or an hour a week may be more time than you have, but tiny plants need all the attention that they can get.

- Consider plant size when planting so that taller growing varieties don't cast smaller types into the shade.

- Use a string line if you want to plant in rows.

- Plant so that the sunlight exposure is even for all rows.

- Allow space between plants so that cultivation is easy.

- Interplant quick growing crops such as rocket, radish and lettuce between slower growing ones. This ensures that the fast growing ones are out of the way by the time the slower growing ones need the space.

- Plant sweet corn in blocks rather than rows to ensure better pollination.

- Don't plant more of any one crop at one time, that cannot be stored or eaten fresh, especially crops such as radish and lettuce.

- When planting reject sickly spindly seedlings.

- Check transplants for diseases, insect damage and mishandling before you buy them.

- Place a few pavers in the garden bed to provide easy access.

- Less frequent, heavy watering is better for the garden than frequent light sprinklings.

- Install a watering system or use drip hoses and connect your watering system to a timing device.